ANGER MANAGEMENT FOR CHRISTIANS

Participant Workbook

A Faith-Based Guide to Understanding and Overcoming Anger through Biblical Principles

DR. ARLEEN A. FULLER, PH.D.

Author: Derek Collins

To order copies of this workbook visit www.thediversioncenter.com

Table of Contents

Proverbs 29:11

"A fool gives full vent to his anger, but a wise man keeps himself under control."

INTRODUCTION

Welcome to anger management. Your counselor/facilitator is here to help you decrease episodes of anger and aggressive behavior. If you want to get the most out of this group, you need to be honest with yourself and deal with the underlying issues that led you to this group.

This group is not designed to attack you. It is designed to help you. Our goal is to deliver information that will help you examine your life and evaluate your choices so you may be a happier, healthier, human being.

Class objectives

- ✓ To help you manage and control your response to anger
- ✓ Evaluate perception, values, thought management, and conditioning
- ✓ Help reduce the number of negative outbursts
- ✓ Prevent emotional hijacking
- ✓ Refer to scripture for guidance and learn positive coping strategies
- ✓ Promote self-awareness, preventative strategies, social skills, and personal development

WHAT IS ANGER?

Anger is a powerful emotion that can take over a person's ability to think rationally. Anger causes the brain to process incoming data as a threat and this triggers the brain to implement the fight or flight response.

Anger can be described as a negative internal feeling state that can range from mild irritation to rage and can be expressed verbally or non-verbally. It's an automatic reaction to any real or imagined insult, frustration, or injustice.

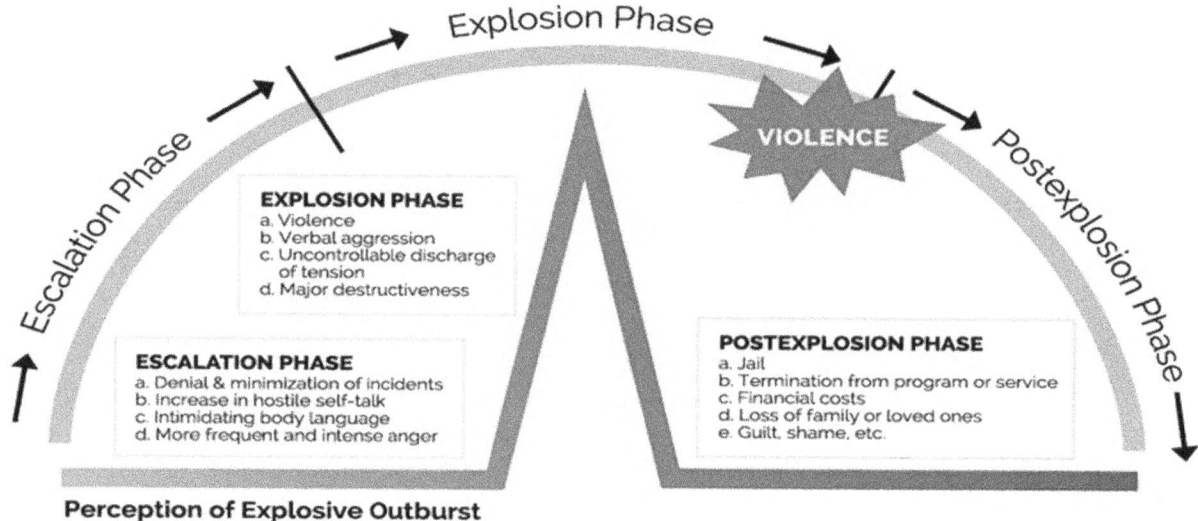

Anger is an emotion that we are born with and it is one of the many emotions that we experience as a human being. We are born with happiness, sadness, anger, etc. Many believe that anger is bad. This is not true. Anger is an emotion that informs us that something is wrong. Anger management teaches us that we have two choices after we get angry. We have a good choice and a bad choice. Anger management teaches us to make good choices.

Negative Aspects of Anger

- ✓ False perceptions of reality can be created
- ✓ Limited views or distorted views can be developed
- ✓ Clouded thinking
- ✓ Lowers IQ

- ✓ It can make one emotionally/spiritually weak
- ✓ Anger can hurt others

Some Physical Symptoms of Anger Related Problems

- ✓ Clenching your jaws or grinding your teeth
- ✓ Headaches
- ✓ Stomach aches
- ✓ Increased and rapid heart rate
- ✓ Sweating, especially your palms
- ✓ Feeling hot in the neck/face
- ✓ Shaking or trembling
- ✓ Dizziness

Anger is a problem when it......

- ✓ Disturbs personal and professional relationships
- ✓ When it is normalized
- ✓ Too intense
- ✓ Leads to aggression
- ✓ Last too long
- ✓ Hurts others

Positive aspects of anger

- ✓ Anger can be used for good
- ✓ Anger can be used as motivational tool
- ✓ Anger can promote change
- ✓ Anger can lead to assertive behavior
- ✓ Anger can help one defend themselves from mistreatment or abuse
- ✓ Anger is a form of self-awareness that informs us that something is wrong

SEEDS OF ANGER

Below is a list of reasons why some people are angry.

Place a checkmark next to any that apply to you.

_____ Family History

_____ Substance Abuse

_____ Poor Financial Management

_____ Societal Influences

_____ Physical Abuse

_____ Jealousy and Envy

_____ Resentment

_____ Lack of Professional Development

_____ Lack of Commitment (quits when times get hard)

_____ Poor Decision Making

_____ Excessive Spending

_____ Poor Values

_____ Lack of Comfort

_____ Hunger

_____ Heat

_____ Poor Mental and Physical Health

_____ Regret

_____ Failure

_____ Working or Living in a Hostile Environment

_____ Poor Self-Talk

_____ Lying to Oneself

_____ Listening to the Wrong People

_____ Limited thinking

_____ Failure to live authentically

_____ Other(s): _____

Proverbs 14:17

"A quick-tempered man acts foolishly, and a man of evil devices is hated."

Ephesians 4:26-32

"Be ye angry, and sin not: let not the sun go down upon your wrath: Neither give place to the devil. Let him that stole steal no more: but rather let him labour, working with his hands the thing which is good, that he may have to give to him that needeth. Let no corrupt communication proceed out of your mouth, but that which is good to the use of edifying, that it may minister grace unto the hearers. And grieve not the holy Spirit of God, whereby ye are sealed unto the day of redemption. Let all bitterness, and wrath, and anger, and clamour, and evil speaking, be put away from you, with all malice:And be ye kind one to another, tenderhearted, forgiving one another, even as God for Christ's sake hath forgiven you."

PERCEPTION

How we view or see things can influence our thought process and behavior. Inaccurate perceptions of situations can lead to negative thinking, negative behavior, and negative consequences. There is power in perception. Have you ever viewed something as hard to achieve and then when you tried it, it was easy? Or have you ever viewed something as easy and it was actually hard? Or have you ever had the wrong perception of someone or something? We have to be mindful of our perceptions. Everything is not always what it seems to be and we need to make sure that we are looking through the right lens.

1. What is your perception of being in anger management? Please be honest.

_____

_____

_____

_____

_____

2. How did you come to this conclusion? Is it based on your personal experience or what others have told you?

_____

_____

_____

_____

_____

3. Do you have the right perception? Are you looking through the right lens?

_____

_____

_____

_____

_____

4. Many people say that "seeing is believing." 2 Corinthians 5:7 states

"For we walk by faith, not by sight." Do we apply both statements to our lives or do we follow one and not the other?

_____

_____

_____

_____

_____

The statement "seeing is believing" is based on perception. There are those that will never manage their anger because they don't see themselves having a problem. They will rationalize or defend their behavior because they perceive it as acceptable. They may even believe or perceive that other people are the ones that have the real problem.

5. What perception do you have of yourself? What do you believe about yourself? Please be honest.

_____

_____

_____

_____

_____

6. Sometimes having the wrong perception can trigger people lose control of their emotions. Has this ever happened to you? If so, what can you do to make sure this doesn't happen again?

_____

_____

_____

_____

7. What is the difference between being rational and irrational?

_____

_____

_____

_____

_____

8. What can you do to make sure you make rational choices?

_____

_____

_____

_____

_____

9. Many people say "I don't care what other people think." But many are lying to themselves. What strategies can you use to keep a positive mindset if someone perceives you the wrong way?

_____

_____

_____

_____

_____

10. If you were failed to manage your anger on a regular basis what would be the possible consequences?

_____

_____

_____

_____

_____

John 10:10

"The thief cometh not, but for to steal, and to kill, and to destroy: I am come that they might have life, and that they might have it more abundantly."

SELF-ACTUALIZATION

Create a plan and write down the things that you can do now to become your ideal self.

_____

_____

_____

_____

_____

_____

_____

_____

_____

_____

_____

_____

_____

_____

_____

_____

_____

_____

_____

_____

_____

_____

_____

_____

_____

_____

PREVENTION PLAN

Prevention Plans are created to assist in monitoring behavior patterns and gives you the ability to make adjustments. This tool will assist you in examining your behavior and creating positive alternative choices when you are triggered to do something negative due to being angry. Please write down your triggers and your usual response to them. After that is complete, write down the same triggers and a positive alternative response for each trigger.

Trigger	Negative Response
Example: Failure	Response: Go get drunk

Trigger	Negative Response
Example: Failure	Response: I'm going to view this as a learning process and I understand that many people fail. Now is not the time to be irrational and find an excuse to drink. I will take a break and do something that improves my mood. When I am ready, I will try again.

Avoiding Triggers

You may have heard some people say "be smart, not strong." If we are smart, we do not have to be strong. This implies that we can avoid returning to negative behavior patterns by using better judgment. Certain people, places, or things can trigger negative behavior patterns. By placing yourself in these situations, it will require you to be strong. Many of us think we are strong, but we are really not.

Choose to be smart and avoid your triggers.

In the boxes below, please list the people, places, and things that you need to avoid.

People	Places	Things

What discussion topics do you need to avoid?

_____

_____

_____

_____

_____

DENIAL

Denial is something that we must address in anger management. There are those in group that will give a million excuses to why they do the things that they do. They will rationalize their behavior and defend choices by bringing up statistics, laws in other countries, scientific studies, etc. Most of them know what they are saying is full of you-know-what. They are not fooling the counselor or the people around them. They are just fooling themselves.

What are you in denial about? Denial can be a seed of anger. Here are a list of things that some people are in denial about:

Relationships	Career Choice
Eating	Fame
Habits	Spending Habits
Getting Older	Illness
Exercising	Work Ethic
Family History	Their Children
School Work	Appearance
Substance Use	

1. Can you add to this list? What are people in denial about?

_____

_____

_____

_____

2. Why do you think some people live in denial?

_____

_____

_____

_____

_____

3. Is this healthy?

Yes or No

4. What are you in denial about? Are you going to stay in denial or change?

_____

_____

_____

_____

_____

5. Does denial truly help you? Please explain

_____

_____

_____

_____

_____

6. What would you like to change? Put a check next to all that apply to you.

_____ Substance Use		_____ Work Environment
_____ Negative Thinking		_____ Commitment
_____ Financial Management		_____ Self-Talk
_____ Excessive Spending		_____ Decision Making
_____ Peer Group		_____ Values
_____ Spouse		_____ Temperament
_____ Abusive Behavior		_____ Education Level
_____ Physical Health		_____ Discipline
_____ Jealousy and Envy		_____ Thought Process
_____ Career		_____ Mental Health
_____ Resentment		_____ Criminal Behavio

STAGES OF CHANGE

Stage 1: Pre-contemplation (Not Ready)

Individuals do not see their behavior as a problem in this stage. Those in the Pre- contemplation stage do not intend to take action in the foreseeable future, even if they have experienced negative consequences for their actions.

Stage 2: Contemplation (Getting Ready)

Contemplation is the stage in which people are aware of the pros and cons of changing their behavior. Instead of defending their behavior, they evaluate, and consider the idea of changing. Continuously weighing the costs and benefits of changing can produce chronic contemplation or procrastination.

Stage 3: Preparation

Preparation is the stage to take action and do specific things that promote change. These individuals have a plan of action, such as going to therapy, talking to their physician, buying a self-help book, scheduling, creating a budget, etc.

Stage 4: Action

Action is the stage in which people have made specific, overt modifications in their lifestyles. Observers from the outside, like friends, relatives, and co-workers will notice that change is occurring. Specific actions are taken to promote lifestyle changes.

Stage 5: Maintenance

Maintenance is the stage in which people have made positive lifestyle choices and have been successful at avoiding relapse. While in the Maintenance stage, people are less tempted to relapse and grow increasingly more confident that they can continue their changes.

What stage of change are you in for the selection that applied to you?

_____ Substance Use	_____ Work Environment
_____ Negative Thinking	_____ Commitment
_____ Financial Management	_____ Self-Talk
_____ Excessive Spending	_____ Decision Making
_____ Peer Group	_____ Values
_____ Spouse	_____ Temperament
_____ Abusive Behavior	_____ Education Level
_____ Physical Health	_____ Discipline
_____ Jealousy and Envy	_____ Thought Process
_____ Career	_____ Mental Health
_____ Resentment	_____ Criminal Behavior

How can you improve your weak areas?

_____

_____

_____

_____

_____

James 2:24-26

"You see then that a man is justified by works, and not by faith only. Likewise, was not Rahab the harlot also justified by works when she received the messengers and sent them out another way? For as the body without the spirit is dead, so faith without works is dead also."

MOTIVATION TO CHANGE

Motivation to change usually occurs when there is a perceived purpose or benefit to change. Many people minimize their behavior, make multiple excuses, or say "Why should I change?" In the back of their minds, they know that change requires work and this might be an uncomfortable adjustment.

Everyone likes a job with benefits. But to get the benefits, you have to be disciplined and do the work. In this section, we want you to weigh the long-term pros and cons of changing your behavior. We want you to find your purpose for doing the work.

Pros	Cons

Pros	Cons

ANGER MANAGEMENT STRATEGIES

- Exercise
- Remove yourself from the event that is triggering you.
- Practice deep breathing and progressive muscle relaxation exercises.
- Change your perception of the situation.
- Listen to music or watch something funny that changes your mood.
- Work on personal and professional goals.
- Try to see the "big picture" and be rational.
- Understand how prescription drugs affect your body.
- Don't engage in conversations with those you are not comfortable with. Example: (politics or religion)
- Do something that makes you feel good.

- Be self-aware and know what you can handle. Place yourself in the best position for success.
- Get adequate food and rest.
- Be financially responsible.
- Let go of the past.
- Stop drug or alcohol use.
- Take alternate routes when dealing with traffic.
- Plan ahead of time
- Self-Care (Massages, Vacations, Grooming)
- Pray
- Prevent yourself from being deprived of food or rest.
- Read Scripture
- Practice being assertive

ASSERTIVENESS

Assertiveness involves standing up for your rights and expressing feelings, thoughts, and beliefs in direct, honest, and appropriate ways that do not disrespect or violate the rights of others. Assertiveness is a part of anger management.

What is assertiveness?

- ✓ Stating your ideas confidently, directly and with clarity
- ✓ Confronting difficult issues in without insulting or putting down others
- ✓ Expressing your concerns, wants or needs

Benefits from being assertive

- ✓ Protects one from being abused or taken advantage of
- ✓ Promotes dialogue and examination of issues
- ✓ Builds self-esteem
- ✓ Clarifies position or stance
- ✓ Increases honesty, requests, refusals
- ✓ Promotes negotiation
- ✓ Decreases regret

Negative forms of assertiveness

- ✓ Manipulation
- ✓ Hostility or Aggressiveness
- ✓ Passive Aggressive

1. What are the benefits of being assertive?

_____

_____

_____

_____

_____

2. How will you deal with someone who is trying to intimidate or control you?

_____

_____

_____

_____

_____

3. Are you willing to defend your beliefs? Why or why not?

_____

_____

_____

_____

_____

4. What is the difference between being assertive and being aggressive?

_____

_____

_____

_____

_____

5. Is sticking up for other people important? Why or why not?

_____

_____

_____

_____

_____

Proverbs 14:29

"He who is slow to anger has great understanding, but he who is quick-tempered exalts folly."

1. How do you deal with anger? Do you fight, run away, or hold things in?

_____

_____

_____

_____

_____

2. What is your best strategy to remove anger that does not involve substance use?

_____

_____

_____

_____

_____

3. What strategies do you use when you are engaged in conflicts with different types of personalities?

- ✓ Those who are aggressive
- ✓ Those who are passive aggressive
- ✓ Those who avoid conflict
- ✓ Those who are silent
- ✓ Those who hold grudges
- ✓ Those who are in power positions

Aggressive _____

Passive Aggressive _____

Those who avoid conflict _____

Those who are silent _____

Those who hold grudges _____

Those who are in power positions _____

PICK YOUR BATTLES

Write down an example of a time that you were emotional about a situation and it ended up making your life more difficult. Were you rational or irrational?

_____

_____

_____

_____

_____

_____

_____

_____

_____

_____

_____

What did you learn from this situation?

_____

_____

_____

_____

_____

_____

_____

_____

_____

_____

_____

James 4: 2

"What causes quarrels and what causes fights among you? Is it not this, that your passions are at war within you? You desire and do not have, so you murder. You covet and cannot obtain, so you fight and quarrel. You do not have, because you do not ask. You ask and do not receive, because you ask wrongly, to spend it on your passions."

Conflict Resolution Model

1. Identify the problem that is causing the conflict. Be specific when identifying the problem.

2. Identify the feelings associated with the conflict.

3. Identify the specific impact of the problem that is causing the conflict.

4. Decide whether to resolve the conflict or let it go. This may be best phrased by the questions, "Is the conflict important enough to bring up? If I do not try to resolve this issue, will it lead to feelings of anger and resentment?" If you decide that the conflict is important enough, then the fifth step is necessary.

5. Address and resolve the conflict.

The A-B-C-D Model

Identify irrational beliefs and dispute them with more rational or realistic perspectives.

A = Activating Situation (Trigger)

B = Belief System

What you tell yourself about the event (self-talk). Your beliefs and expectations of others.

C = Consequence

How you feel about the event based on your self-talk.

D = Dispute:

Examine your beliefs and expectations. Are they unrealistic or irrational?

Barriers to Listening

- ✓ Shaming, Ridiculing, or Labeling
- ✓ Withdrawing, Distracting, Humoring, or Changing the Subject
- ✓ Warning or Threatening
- ✓ Ordering, Directing, or Commanding
- ✓ Lecturing or Arguing
- ✓ Moralizing or Preaching,

- ✓ Judging, Criticizing, or Blaming
- ✓ Agreeing, Approving, or Praising
- ✓ Interpreting or Analyzing

Proverbs 16:32

"He who is slow to anger is better than the mighty, and he who rules his spirit, than he who captures a city."

MOOD MANAGEMENT STRATEGIES

Music – Listen to enjoyable music. Listening to your favorite songs can improve your mood. Music is a powerful tool that has been used in movies to enhance emotions of fear, joy, sadness, excitement, etc. Imagine watching a scary movie without background music or sound effects. It wouldn't be as scary. You can use music to change your mood.

Nostalgia – Reminisce about happy times in your past. Review old pictures, movies, or television series that you used to enjoy. Do things that you used to enjoy, that you don't do now.

Self-Care – Take care of yourself. Get a massage, pedicure, manicure, etc. Go on vacation and eat healthy food. Exercise to increase your production of endorphins. With high endorphin levels, we feel less pain and fewer negative effects of stress. Endorphins have been suggested as modulators of the so-called "runner's high" that athletes achieve with prolonged exercise.

Self-Talk – Monitor or be mindful of what you say to yourself. Try to be positive and say things to yourself that uplift you instead of bring you down. Negative self- talk is not healthy and can destroy your life.

Journaling – Write down what is on your mind. By journaling, you can evaluate your life and express yourself honestly. Act out your emotions on paper. Later, you can review your entries and decide if you were being rational or being irrational.

You can review your journal to remind yourself of previous accomplishments, lessons, and how you have overcome obstacles. Journaling is a great tool for personal growth.

Change Environment – Some people live, work, or go to school in negative environments. You would be surprised how exposure to different people, places, or things can improve your life. If you are in a negative environment, consider changing it to a positive one. Your odds of living a happy life increase when you are in a positive environment.

Counseling – Sometimes people become overwhelmed and are unable to cope with life's stressors. If this is the case for you, consider seeing a counselor. A professional counselor can assist you with challenging issues in your life.

Receiving guidance from a neutral party who has no emotional attachment to the situation may bring clarity.

Improve Self-talk – The act or practice of talking to oneself, either aloud or silently (mentally). Self-talk can have a great impact on your self-esteem and confidence.

There is positive and negative self-talk and they both have an impact on how you feel.

Stress Prevention Strategies – Do things ahead of time in order to prevent future stressful events from occurring. We want you to anticipate needs. Examples include: budgeting, planning ahead, paying bills on time, leaving early from work to avoid traffic, getting things done before you are asked, telling people "no," etc.

Song of Solomon 4:7

"You are altogether beautiful, my love; there is no flaw in you."

SELF-ESTEEM

Self-esteem is a term in psychology to reflect a person's overall evaluation or appraisal of his or her own worth. Low self-esteem affects both males and females. Although self-esteem is rarely discussed as a male issue, men and boys are affected by low self-esteem.

1. How does someone with low self-esteem behave?

_____

_____

_____

_____

_____

2. How does someone with healthy self-esteem behave?

_____

_____

_____

_____

_____

3. What is the difference between healthy self-esteem and arrogance?

_____

_____

_____

_____

_____

4. Sometimes those with low self-esteem try to bully, abuse, or talk down to others. Why do you think they do this? Have you ever experienced this? If so, how did this affect you or others?

_____

_____

_____

_____

_____

5. How do you deal with bullies at the workplace?

_____

_____

_____

_____

_____

Strategies to Improve Self-Esteem

✓ Pursue easy goals

Start with something you can accomplish easily. When we achieve small successes, it builds our confidence and momentum to go after bigger goals.

✓ Socialize

Get out of the house and practice your communication and interpersonal skills. Don't be afraid to engage in conversations. Others may be just as nervous as we are and do not express it. We are not alone. Some people are magicians and we only see what they allow us to see.

✓ Face your fears

It is important for us to face our fears so we can grow. By repeatedly facing our fears our irrational beliefs diminish and we gain confidence and courage.

✓ Build on your strengths

Do things on a regular basis that comes natural for you. Doing things that you are good at reinforces belief in your abilities and strengths. You can also add to your skills by taking advanced coursework or certification training in your field of study.

✓ Stop comparing yourself to others

Stop comparing yourself to other people. Low self-esteem stems from the feeling of being inferior. For example, if you were the only person in the world, do you think you could have low self-esteem? Self-esteem only comes into the picture when there are other people around us and we perceive that we are inferior. Don't worry about what your neighbor is doing. Accept that it'll serve you more to just go down your own path at your own pace rather than to compare yourself.

✓ Know thyself

Know who you are and what you need to improve on. Your self-esteem is based on the major categories of your life. Write down all the major categories of your life (e.g., health, finance, relationships, etc.). Then rate yourself on a scale of 1-10 in each area. Work on the lowest numbered category first. Each area affects the other areas. The more you build up each area of your life, the higher your overall self-esteem.

✓ Create a vision of yourself

Use your imagination and create an image of yourself as the confident and self-assured person you aspire to become. When you are this person, how will you feel? How will others perceive you? What does your body language look like? How will you talk? Feel the emotions, experiences, and daydream about your ideal life.

✓ Help others achieve their goals

Helping others achieve their goals can be fulfilling. It puts a smile on their face and can make you feel good as well. Plus if you help them with their goals, maybe they will help you with your goals.

✓ Create a plan

Having a goal is not enough. You need to have an action plan. Get moving and follow the steps that you need to take to achieve your goals.

✓ Get motivated

Be purpose driven. Have a reason why you are doing something. Associate yourself with people or things that inspire you. If you desire to be motivated, use this formula: High Emotion + Strong Purpose = Motivation

✓ Improve self-talk

Sometimes we have internal thoughts that are negative and irrational. We have to manage our self-talk and reinforce positive thoughts that improve our perspective. Internally, we can say good things about ourselves and build a positive image.

✓ Be positive

There are many people that allow negative energy to transfer into their lives. Know that it is okay to smile and people are attracted to happy people. Do not allow negative people to transfer their energy into you. Just because they are mad does not mean that you have to be. You are in control of your perceptions. There are no benefits to being negative.

PERSONAL ADVICE

Imagine that you are five years in the future and you have to write a letter to your present self. What advice would you give?

_____

_____

_____

_____

_____

_____

_____

_____

_____

_____

_____

_____

_____

_____

_____

_____

_____

_____

_____

_____

_____

_____

_____

_____

_____

_____

_____

_____

_____

_____

_____

_____

_____

_____

_____

_____

_____

_____

_____

_____

_____

_____

_____

_____

_____

_____

_____

_____

Colossians 3:13

"Bearing with one another and, if one has a complaint against another, forgiving each other; as the Lord has forgiven you, so you also must forgive."

FORGIVENESS

Forgiveness is one of the hardest things to do. Letting go of the past and removing resentment is healthy. There are no benefits to holding on to grudges and past hurts. It's like driving a car while looking through the rearview mirror. Eventually, you will crash.

1. Who do you need to forgive and why?

Family   Friends Co-workers   Spouse Children   Yourself

_____

_____

_____

_____

_____

2. Do you forgive and forget? Or do you forgive and not forget?

_____

_____

_____

_____

_____

3. Is making amends important to you? If so, who do you need to say sorry to, and why?

_____

_____

_____

_____

_____

4. What does true forgiveness look, act, and sound like?

_____

_____

_____

_____

5. After you forgive someone, does that mean you should still associate yourself with them?

_____

_____

_____

_____

Deuteronomy 28:1-2

"And it shall come to pass, if thou shalt hearken diligently unto the voice of the LORD thy God to observe and to do all His commandments which I command thee this day, that the LORD thy God will set thee on high above all nations of the earth; and all these blessings shall come on thee and overtake thee, if thou shalt hearken unto the voice of the LORD thy God:"

LIVING BY PRINCIPLES

It is important to have principles. Principles are the governors of your values and protect the things that you care about the most. The principles that you create will help you when you need to make tough decisions.

Values

Freedom

Principle: I do not hang out with people who sell or use drugs.

This protects my freedom, life, and family.

Career

Principle: I attend trainings quarterly to improve my skill level.

This helps my career and shows that I am committed.

Reputation

Principle: I have a strong work ethic and provide quality service.

This protects my reputation and increases my earning potential.

List the things that you value.

1._____

2._____

3._____

4._____

Now write down principles that protect those values.

1._____

_____

_____

2._____

_____

_____

3._____

_____

_____

4._____

_____

_____

BELIEF AND SELF-IMAGE

What is your overall view of yourself physically, emotionally, and intellectually?

Physically I am:

_____   _____

_____   _____

_____   _____

_____   _____

Emotionally I am:

_____   _____

_____   _____

_____   _____

_____   _____

Intellectually I am:

_____   _____

_____   _____

_____   _____

Spiritually I am:

_____   _____

_____   _____

_____   _____

_____   _____

Write down a list of "shoulds" that you have based on your family, friends, culture, spirituality, media, music, school system, and any other areas. Which of these beliefs are rational and which are irrational? Place an "R" next the beliefs that you think are rational and an "I" next to the beliefs that you deem irrational. Place an "X" next to the statements that describe who you are currently.

		R or I	I am
Example:	I should be skinny	__R__	__X__
	I should be perfect	__I__	_____
	I should be married by now	__I__	_____
	I should get all A's	__R__	_____

I should _____   _____   _____

I should _____   _____   _____

I should _____   _____   _____

I should _____   _____   _____

I should _____   _____   _____

I should _____   _____   _____

I should _____   _____   _____

I should _____   _____   _____

I should _____   _____   _____

I should _____   _____   _____

Write down as many great things about yourself that you can think of in the next 2 minutes.

_____   _____

_____   _____

_____   _____

_____   _____

_____   _____

_____   _____

_____   _____

Write down as many not-so-great things about yourself that you can think of in the next 2 minutes.

_____   _____

_____   _____

_____   _____

_____   _____

_____   _____

_____   _____

_____   _____

Now analyze your two lists. Was it more difficult to write one list than the other? Which list is longer? Why do you think that is?

_____   _____

_____   _____

_____   _____

_____   _____

_____   _____

_____   _____

_____   _____

Write a list of things that people have told you about yourself. Place an "X" next to the statements that you either agree or disagree with.

Example:	Agree	Disagree
I am an excellent writer.	__X__	_____
I am lazy.	__X__	_____
_____	_____	_____

_____   _____   _____

_____   _____   _____

_____   _____   _____

_____   _____   _____

_____   _____   _____

Write a list of things that you believe people think about you. Place an "X" next to the statements that you either agree or disagree with.

Finish the following statement:

People believe that I am: Agree   Disagree

_____   _____   _____

_____   _____   _____

_____   _____   _____

_____   _____   _____

_____   _____   _____

_____   _____   _____

_____   _____   _____

_____   _____   _____

What does God say about you?

Please open your Bible and fill the blanks with scriptures about what God says about you. (KJV)

1. Peter 2:9

_____

_____

_____

2. 2 Corinthians 5:17

_____

_____

_____

3.Romans 8:17

_____

_____

_____

4. 1 Corinthians 6:19

_____

_____

_____

5. Romans 8:2

_____

_____

_____

CONTROLLING YOUR MOUTH

Proverbs 21:23

"Whoever keeps his mouth and his tongue keeps himself out of trouble."

Ephesians 4:29

"Let no corrupting talk come out of your mouths, but only such as is good for building up, as fits the occasion, that it may give grace to those who hear."

Psalm 34:13

"Keep your tongue from evil and your lips from speaking deceit."

Proverbs 17:28

"Even a fool who keeps silent is considered wise; when he closes his lips, he is deemed intelligent."

Titus 3:2

"To speak evil of no one, to avoid quarreling, to be gentle, and to show perfect courtesy toward all people."

Proverbs 18:21

"Death and life are in the power of the tongue, and those who love it will eat its fruits."

Sometimes it's not what you say, but how you _____

FAMILY DRAMA

1. How has your family affected your emotions?

_____

_____

_____

_____

_____

2. How has your family influenced your relationships with others?

_____

_____

_____

_____

_____

3. Which family member can "push your buttons" the most? What do they do?

_____

_____

_____

_____

_____

_____

_____

_____

_____

4. What strategies do other people use in your family to deal with the person mentioned on the previous page?

_____

_____

5. Do they push your buttons because you keep responding to it? How can you change the effect that it has on you?

_____

_____

_____

_____

6. How has family secrets affected your life positively or negatively?

_____

_____

_____

_____

_____

_____

_____

_____

_____

7. Is denial about substance, sexual, verbal, or physical abuse acceptable within the family? Should this history of behavior be hidden from family members? Why or why not?

_____

_____

_____

_____

8. Should accomplishments, awards, promotions, or scholarships be hidden from family members? Why or why not?

_____

_____

9. How can you improve your family?

_____

_____

_____

_____

10. Is family something that you value? If so, in what ways do you show that you value your family? Are you improving your family or are you keeping the family drama alive?

_____

_____

_____

_____

11. Would you raise your children the same way your parents raised you? If not, what changes would you make?

_____

_____

_____

_____

Ephesians 4:31 -32

"Let all bitterness, and wrath, and anger, and clamour, and evil speaking, be put away from you, with all malice: And be ye kind one to another, tenderhearted, forgiving one another, even as God for Christ's sake hath forgiven you."

LET IT GO

1. What is the purpose of holding on to the past?

_____

_____

_____

_____

_____

2. Where does "holding on to the past" get you?

_____

_____

_____

_____

_____

3. Is your past affecting you presently? If so, how?

_____

_____

_____

_____

4. Does holding on to negative things in your past benefit you in any way?

_____

_____

_____

_____

_____

5. Seriously, does being negative or pessimistic lead to positive results?

_____

_____

_____

_____

_____

6. If no, why do people continue to do it?

_____

_____

_____

_____

_____

7. What are the characteristics of victims?

_____

_____

_____

_____

_____

8. Do those characteristics describe you? Would you like to be held in eternal bondage by your past?

_____

_____

_____

_____

_____

Romans 8:37 _____

Proverbs 14:29

"Whoever is patient has great understanding, but one who is quick-tempered displays folly."

DELAYED GRATIFICATION

1. How has instant gratification affected your life?

_____

_____

_____

_____

_____

2. What are the benefits of delayed gratification?

_____

_____

_____

_____

_____

3. What are the cons of instant gratification?

_____

_____

_____

_____

_____

4. Are fast things good for you? Please explain.

_____

_____

_____

_____

_____

5. Do good things come to those who wait? Please explain.

_____

_____

_____

_____

_____

2 Timothy 1:7

"For God has not given us a spirit of fear; but of power, love, and a sound mind."

FEAR

Many people are controlled by fear. These fears can manifest into anger and impulse-control problems. FEAR is irrational and it stands for: false existence appearing real.

1. What are you afraid of?

_____

_____

_____

_____

_____

2. What is your greatest fear?

_____

_____

_____

_____

_____

3. What has fear stopped you from doing?

_____

_____

_____

_____

_____

4. How has fear impacted your life?

_____

_____

_____

_____

_____

5. What does God say about fear? Write down the scriptures below.

_____

_____

_____

_____

_____

CONSEQUENCES OF POOR ANGER MANAGEMENT

- ✓ Expulsion from school
- ✓ Loss of time
- ✓ Loss of respect
- ✓ Loss of relationships
- ✓ Added stress
- ✓ Probation
- ✓ Community Service
- ✓ Loss of freedom
- ✓ Loss of money
- ✓ Health problems
- ✓ Loss of professional licenses
- ✓ Public humiliation
- ✓ Diminished reputation
- ✓ Loss of property
- ✓ Criminal record
- ✓ Court fees, fines, etc.
- ✓ Employment loss
- ✓ Loss of citizenship/residency
- ✓ Embarrassment
- ✓ Guilt
- ✓ Trauma

Financial Consequences

Fines $ _____

Income lost from not working $ _____

Legal Fees (Probation/Court/Lawyer) $ _____

Anger Management Evaluation $ _____

Anger Management Classes $ _____

Childcare $ _____

Gas $ _____

Food bought while taking classes $ _____

Loss of wages $ _____

Repair bills or restitution $ _____

TOTAL MONEY LOST $ _____

Hours in court   _____

Hours in probation   _____

Hours doing community service   _____

Hours in jail   _____

Hours in class   _____

Other hours lost   _____

TOTAL TIME LOST   _____

TIME x HOURLY WAGE = VALUE OF TIME LOST

_____ X $ _____ = $ _____

VALUE OF TIME LOST $ _____

VALUE OF TIME LOST + TOTAL MONEY LOSS= $ _____

IS IT WORTH IT? _____

John 8:32

"And ye shall know the truth, and the truth shall make you free."

TRUTHFULNESS

1. Can women handle the truth? Why or why not?

_____

_____

_____

_____

_____

2. Can men handle the truth? Why or why not?

_____

_____

_____

_____

_____

3. What are things that women lie about?

_____

_____

_____

_____

4. What are things that men lie about?

_____

_____

_____

_____

5. Who are better liars? Women or men?

_____

_____

_____

_____

_____

6. How do women lie differently than men? How do they cover it up? What tactics do they use?

_____

_____

_____

_____

_____

7. Do you respect liars? Why or why not?

_____

_____

_____

_____

_____

8. Do you lie to yourself? If so, why?

_____

_____

_____

_____

_____

9. What is a purpose of a lie?

_____

_____

_____

_____

_____

10. How have lies hurt you in the past?

_____

_____

_____

_____

_____

11. Strip away your ego, defenses, and lies you tell yourself. Truly, who are you?

_____

_____

_____

_____

_____

_____

Galatians 6:7

"Be not deceived; God is not mocked: for whatsoever a man soweth, that shall he also reap."

DECISION TREE

In life, we are required to make a lot of decisions, both big and small. Each choice we make will have a ripple effect on many different aspects of our life that we may have failed to consider. This is why it is very important to evaluate our choices in order to create the best possible outcomes.

Creating a decision tree helps you see the possible ripple effects of your choices.

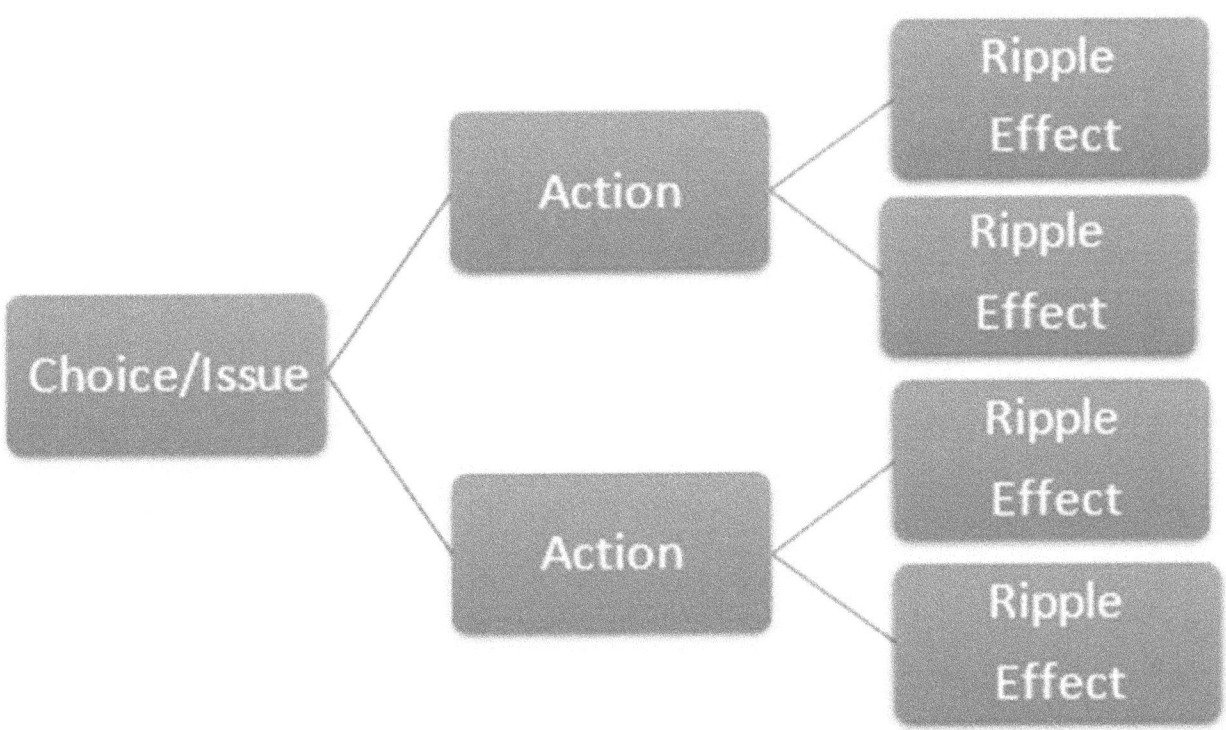

Sample Decision Tree

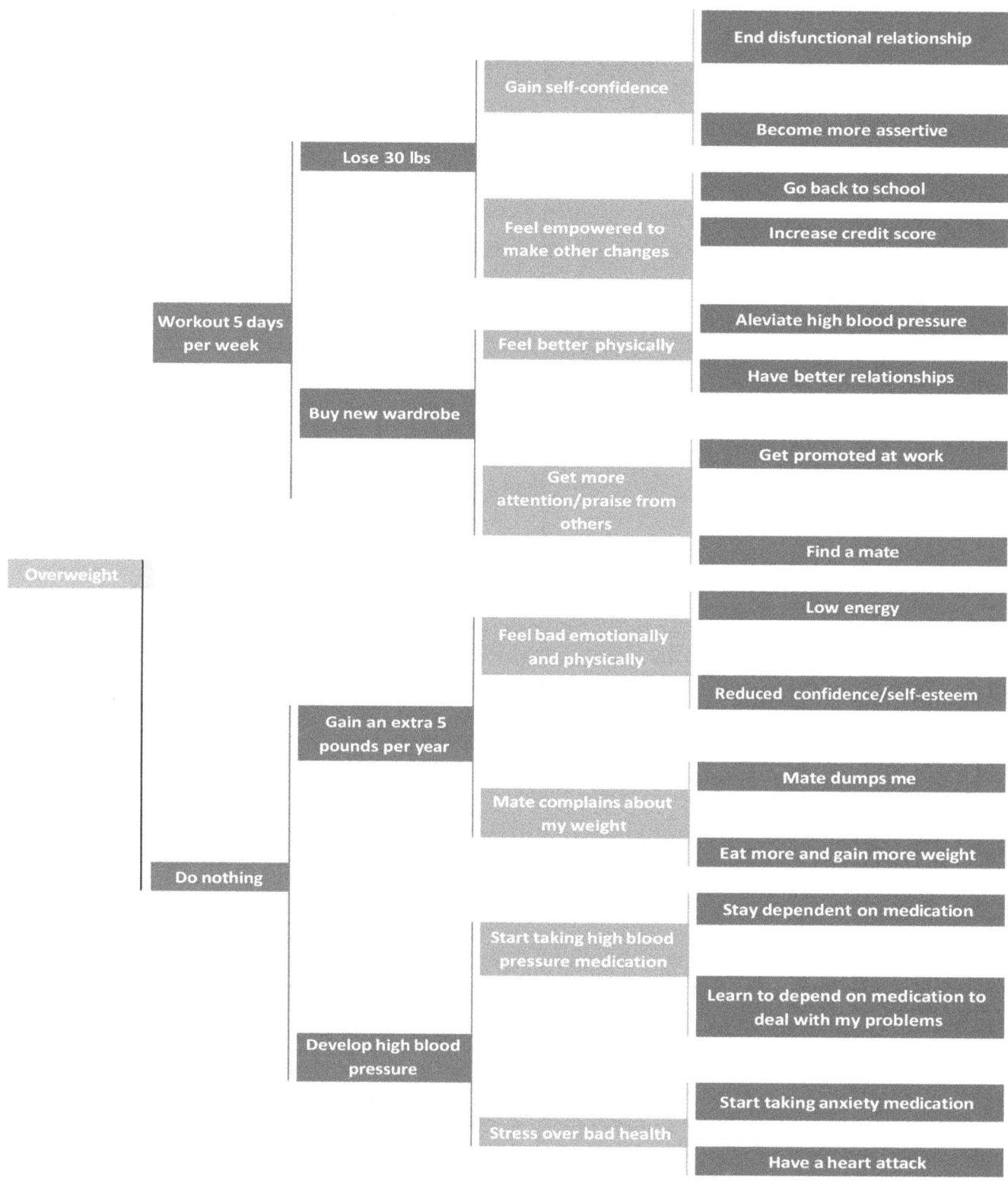

Please create your own decision tree and evaluate your choices on this page.

SELF-AWARENESS

1. What makes you feel happy, relaxed, and fulfilled?

_____

_____

_____

_____

2. What are the top three distractions or weaknesses that keep you from achieving your goals? How will you remove these weaknesses or distractions?

_____

_____

_____

_____

3. What are your strengths? Are there other skills that you need to develop? If so, what are they?

_____

_____

_____

_____

4. Pretend that you were told by your doctor that you had five years to live. How would you change your life? Would you do anything differently?

_____

_____

_____

_____

_____

5. What do you want to be known for? What kind of legacy will you leave behind?

_____

_____

_____

_____

_____

6. Describe the characteristics of your ideal mate. What kind of personality does he/she have? What are his/her physical characteristics? What are deal breakers for you?

Personality	Physical Features	Deal Breakers	Other

7. What was the best birthday you ever had? What did you do and who was there?

_____

_____

_____

_____

_____

8. Who do you admire and respect? What qualities do they have and what do you need to do to get those same qualities?

1. Name: _____Relationship: _____

Qualities: _____

2. Name: _____Relationship: _____

Qualities: _____

9. If you could be any fictional character, who would you be and why?

_____

_____

10. If you had a million dollars right now, how would you spend or invest it? Be specific.

CREDIT

So what is credit anyway? In essence, credit is any form of delayed payment. It allows one party (the debtor or borrower) to receive money, goods, or services from another party (the creditor or lender) without having to pay up front.

Instead there is an agreement based on trust that the borrower will either pay or return the materials (or other materials of equal value) at a later date. The cost of credit comes in the form of a predetermined rate of interest that is applied to the amount borrowed and will accrue until the debt has been paid.

Common forms of credit include:

Mortgages

Personal loans

Credit Cards

Store Cards

Automobile loans

Credit bureaus collect information from various sources regarding your borrowing and bill-paying habits and create a report based on these findings. A credit score is a number that represents your credit worthiness. It is formulated based on your credit report. The most common credit scores are FICO scores. FICO scores range from 300 – 850. The higher the score, the better your credit. Your credit score is used to determine whether you are worthy of credit, to determine interest rates, and assess your ability to pay back loans. In essence, your past behavior is used to predict your future behavior. Because credit is based on trust and your previous financial behavior, it is very important to create a flawless track record of bill paying activity.

1. Do you know your credit score? If so, what is it?

_____

_____

2. When was the last time you checked your credit score and credit report?

_____

_____

3. Do you typically pay your bills on time? Why or why not?

_____

_____

4. How many lines of credit do you have open (credit cards, loans, etc.)?

_____

_____

5. Are your credit cards maxed out? If so, why?

_____

_____

6. Do you pay the minimum amount allowed? If so, why?

_____

_____

7. How soon do you think you will be able to pay off your credit cards?

The United States has 3 national credit bureaus:

Equifax

Experian

TransUnion

8. Do you have a plan in place to pay off your debts? If so, what is it?

_____

_____

9. How can you improve your credit? (FYI, having no credit is bad credit)

_____

_____

Romans 13:8

"Let no debt remain outstanding, except the continuing debt to love one another, for whoever loves others has fulfilled the law."

PERSONAL BUDGET

Many people become angry, depressed, or stressed out due to poor financial management. On this page, create a monthly budget for yourself based on your current income.

Mortgage/Rent: _____

Credit Card: _____

Insurance: _____

Entertainment/Self Care: _____

Utilities: _____

Clothing: _____

Cell Phone: _____

Gas: _____

Internet: _____

Misc.: _____

Groceries: _____

Savings: _____

Money In	**-**	**Money Out**	**=**	**Money Left**
_____	-	_____	=	_____

Proverbs 13:11

"Dishonest money dwindles away, but whoever gathers money little by little makes it grow."

Notes:

_____

_____

_____

_____

_____

_____

_____

Ecclesiastes 7:9

"Do not be eager in your heart to be angry, for anger resides in the bosom of fools."

AMYGDALA HIJACKING

Amygdala hijack describes a situation when a person responds inappropriately based on emotional rather than intellectual factors. The amygdala is the emotional center of the human brain and makes quick responses when a person is threatened. An inappropriate emotional response to a perceived threat is called an amygdala hijack.

The process for the amygdala's response is to: Act→ Feel→Think or Feel→Act→Think.

We want you to: Think→Act→Feel

The amygdala is the part of the brain that protects us from threats. It is considered to be used as a survival mechanism during extreme stimulus or triggers. The prefrontal cortex is the part of the brain where conscious control and decision making processes occur.

During low to moderate stressful events, the prefrontal cortex will calm amygdala down and consider the pros and cons of taking actions. When the stimulus is extreme, the amygdala will shut down the prefrontal cortex function and take over to protect us from threats.

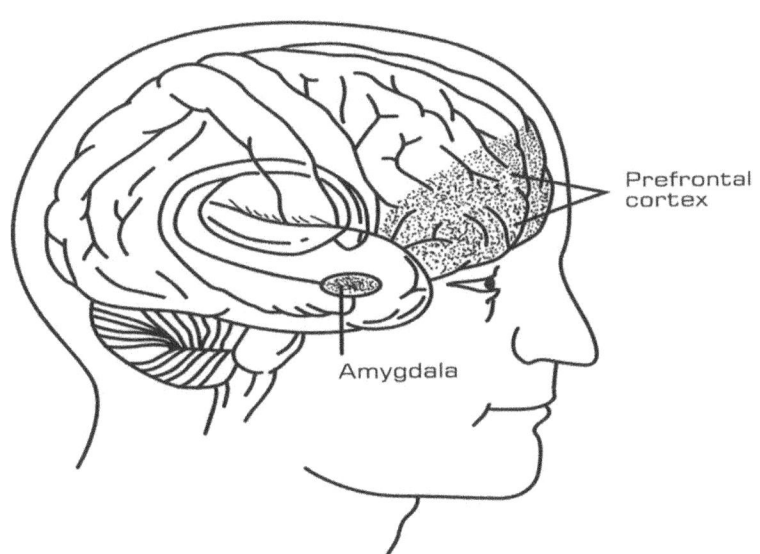

Prefrontal cortex

Amygdala

Unfortunately, many people who suffer from chronic anger perceive low to moderate events as extreme events and activate un-necessary flight or fight responses. "Flight or fight" refers to building up energy to run away, or building up energy to fight. Continuous activation of this process can lead to chronic health problems and negative life experiences.

DECISION-MAKING SCENARIOS

Behavior is developed through our values, principles and the consequences of our actions. Each decision or choice that you make has a ripple effect. We would like for you to practice your decision-making skills while being exposed to emotionally-charged scenarios. There are no right or wrong answers. We just want you to practice making decisions while being emotionally charged.

If you want to get better at singing, public speaking, driving a car, painting, or doing some other skill, you need to practice. People who live the best lives make the best decisions. We want you to make the best decisions for your life.

On the next page, there is a series of scenarios for you to evaluate. Please have a response for each scenario listed. Please keep it real and don't give answers that you think your group or counselor want to hear. Remember this is a judgment-free zone.

Scenario # 1

School is about to start and you just bought some new school clothes for your daughter. While she waits at the bus stop, a neighborhood bully rips her clothes and harasses her. Your daughter reports this back to you and you find out that this bully's parent is your supervisor at your job. How do you handle this situation?

_____

_____

_____

_____

_____

Scenario # 2

Your mom is single and she is dating someone who is the same age as you. They invite you to dinner where he proposes to her and she gladly accepts. They have been only dating for a month. Later that evening, he comes to you and asks for your blessing and support of his marriage to your mom. How do you handle this situation?

_____

_____

Scenario # 3

You are a mother/father of three children. You're offered a spot on a popular reality show. The pay is $200,000 per episode. The show is very popular and known for having a lot of fights, arguments, and undignified behavior. In order to be on the show you must behave the same way (i.e., argue and fight, tell the world all your deep dark secrets, sexualize yourself, let people disrespect you, disrespect others and show the worst sides of yourself). What would you do?

_____

_____

_____

_____

Scenario # 4

You're watching the news and you see video footage of a man that is wanted by the police for murdering a woman and burning her body on the side of the road near your house. The man looks exactly like your brother. Just a week before, on the night of the murder, your brother came to your house looking worried and asking for a gas can. Although you didn't give him your gas can, you noticed later on that it was missing. What would you do?

_____

_____

_____

_____

Scenario # 5

You are at a family gathering and your cousin has brought his new girlfriend. You notice that he is being verbally abusive to her (i.e., calling her out of her name, saying disrespectful things and threatening to beat her up). What do you do?

_____

_____

_____
_____
_____

Scenario # 6

You are on probation and your supervisor needs a ride home. He uses cocaine on a regular basis and is known to have cocaine on him at all times. Do you give him a ride home?

_____
_____
_____
_____
_____

Scenario # 7

You are struggling financially and your neighbor is "getting over" because she is getting disability, food stamps, and a tax return for three kids that are not hers.

Plus she has a babysitting business next door and is not licensed by the state to run a daycare.

    1) Do you report her?

    2) Do you blackmail her to get a cut of her money?

    3) Do you ignore the situation and mind your business?

    4) Other _____

Scenario # 8

You get laid off from work and receive your final check. With this check you now have a total of $800 left to your name to pay your $700 rent, $300 car note, and

$200 in utility bills. It is your daughter's sixth birthday next week. How do you handle this situation? What will be your strategy?

_____
_____
_____
_____
_____

Scenario # 9

You are hanging out at your friend's house watching football and he decides to invite more people over to watch the game. These are all of the people that you used to drink and drug with before you entered treatment. How will you handle this situation?

_____

_____

_____

_____

_____

Scenario # 10

You and your co-worker were given a joint project to complete but your co-worker was lazy and you ended up doing all the work. When it was time to present to your boss your co-worker took over the presentation and made it seem like they were the leader on it. Your boss then praised your co-worker and said nothing to you.

How do you handle this situation?

_____

_____

_____

_____

_____

MINDSET MAINTENANCE

✓ Know your triggers and stay away from them.

✓ Find alternate ways to cope.

✓ Go to counseling for un-resolved issues like grief, depression, anger, anxiety, substance use, or a gambling or sex addiction.

✓ Engage in activities that improve your mood (manage your emotions).

✓ Do positive things that you used to enjoy that you don't do now (nostalgia, music, hobbies, old television shows).

✓ Try something new and gain exposure to exciting things that interest you.

✓ Resolve personal issues with family, friends and coworkers.

✓ Be assertive and do not be afraid to tell people "no."

✓ Be aware and adjust your behavior patterns.

✓ Stay away from negative influences.

✓ Develop an action plan to improve emotionally, physically, and financially.

✓ Understand the long-term consequences of your actions and how it will affect you personally, professionally, and emotionally.

✓ Practice delayed gratification.

✓ Create a budget for yourself and only buy what you need and save for the future.

✓ When you have the urge to engage in negative behaviors, know that you have a choice. You are not on auto-pilot and you can control your behavior.

✓ Go to school and improve your marketability by earning a degree, trade, or license in a specialized field. Work on professional goals.

✓ Exercise regularly and try to get sunlight as much as possible to increase endorphins.

✓ Do positive things and engage in legal experiences that make you happy.

✓ Develop a relapse prevention plan. Pre-plan on how you are going to respond to stress, anxiety, failure, and mistakes in a positive manner that lead to long-term success.

✓ Go to church and get spiritual guidance.

TIME MANAGEMENT

Goals   Priority   Deadline

1. _____   _____   _____

2. _____   _____   _____

3. _____   _____   _____

4. _____   _____   _____

5. _____   _____   _____

Time   Activity   Time   Activity

_____   _____   _____   _____

Monday

_____   _____   _____   _____

_____   _____   _____   _____

_____   _____   _____   _____

_____   _____   _____   _____

Time   Activity   Time   Activity

_____   _____   _____   _____

Tuesday

_____   _____   _____   _____

_____   _____   _____   _____

_____   _____   _____   _____

_____   _____   _____   _____

Time   Activity   Time   Activity

_____ _____   _____ _____

Wednesday

_____   _____   _____   _____

_____   _____   _____   _____

_____   _____   _____   _____

_____   _____   _____   _____

Time   Activity   Time   Activity

_____ _____   _____ _____

Thursday

_____   _____   _____   _____

_____   _____   _____   _____

_____   _____   _____   _____

_____   _____   _____   _____

Time   Activity   Time   Activity

_____ _____   _____ _____

Friday

_____   _____   _____   _____

_____   _____   _____   _____

_____   _____   _____   _____

Time	Activity	Time	Activity
___	___	___	___
___	___	___	___

Saturday

___	___	___	___
___	___	___	___
___	___	___	___
___	___	___	___

Time	Activity	Time	Activity
___	___	___	___

Sunday

___	___	___	___
___	___	___	___
___	___	___	___
___	___	___	___

Time	Activity	Time	Activity
___	___	___	___

Philippians 4:13

"I can do all things through Christ who strengthens me."

SETTING GOALS

Write a list of short-term and long-term goals that you would like to accomplish.

_____

_____

_____

_____

_____

_____

_____

_____

_____

_____

Transform your list of goals into SMART goals by answering the following questions. Start with the first goal listed above.

Goal:

_____

_____

Specific: What specifically do you want to do?

_____

_____

_____

_____

Measurable: How will you measure your success? How much? How many?

_____

_____

Attainable: Is it in your power to accomplish this goal?

_____

_____

Relevant: Is this goal consistent with your other goals and plans.

_____

_____

Time-bound: What is the established deadline that will create a reasonable sense of urgency for you to complete the goal?

_____

_____

SMART Goal:

_____

_____

_____

_____

_____

PROFESSIONAL DEVELOPMENT

What can you specialize in that makes you different from the crowd? What special skill, niche, or talent can you develop that will put you in demand?

Homework Assignment:

Go on the internet and search for careers that require a special skill or training that you would be willing to commit to. Look for something that most people are not doing or thinking about. Look for apprenticeship and certification programs. Do not be discouraged if it requires you to jump through a lot of hoops. This element is created to weed out competition and the people who are not serious.

Sample Careers:

Food Stylist	Deep Sea Welding	Linguistics Specialist
Trauma Cleanup	Polygraph Examiner	Millwright
Fusion Scientist	Cremator	Mediator
Kinesics Expert	Master Penman	Foley Artist

List the careers that you are interested in

_____

_____

_____

_____

_____

What was cool in High School is not cool in adulthood. Many people learn this lesson the hard way and end up being angry due to regret. Successful people tend to sacrifice time, money, and their wants to gain what they need for long-term success. They choose to give up toxic lifestyles, friends, and environments to live a fulfilled life. Others choose another path and end up suffering throughout adulthood because of poor decision making. When their back is against the wall, or when a crisis emerges, they have to rely on doing something that can potentially put them in a worse situation than before. Who will you decide to be? Will you be the person who chooses to sacrifice their wants for their needs, or the person who sacrifices their needs for their wants?

1. What is the difference between a want and a need?

_____

_____

_____

_____

_____

2. What is your ideal career and what steps do you need to take today to get there?

_____

_____

_____

_____

3. Who or what do you need to remove from your life to achieve this goal?

_____

_____

_____

_____

4. In your city or state who is the leader in your field of choice? Would you allow them to mentor you?

_____

_____

_____

_____

5. What is your life's purpose? If you do not know, consider gaining exposure to different people, places, and things so you can find out what you're really good at. You could be a natural violin player but wouldn't even know it because you have never touched a violin.

_____

_____

_____

6. What lifestyle choices do you need to give up to improve your health?

_____

_____

_____

_____

_____

7. What sacrifices can you make right now to achieve long-term success?

_____

_____

_____

_____

_____

1 Corinthians 6:19-20

"Do you not know that your bodies are temples of the Holy Spirit, who is in you, whom you have received from God? You are not your own; you were bought at a price. Therefore honor God with your bodies."

SELF-CARE

There are those in this world who fail to take care of themselves. Due to this, they suffer at work, have poor relationships, live shorter lives, use illegal drugs to cope, etc. It is important that we take care of ourselves. Check the things that you would like to do to improve your self-care.

_____ Massages		_____ Vacation	
_____ Manicures		_____ Counseling	
_____ Pedicures		_____ Improve Living Environment	
_____ Facials		_____ Improve Work Environment	
_____ Staycation		_____ Buy New Clothes	
_____ Alone time		_____ Sleep	
_____ Sunlight		_____ Read	
_____ Exercise		_____ Improve Eating Habits	
_____ Be in Nature		_____ Hobbies	
_____ Socialize		_____ Other	

BELIEVE IN YOURSELF

If you do all the activities in this book and understand the concepts presented, but fail to believe in yourself, this will be a waste of your time. How can you believe in God but not believe in yourself?

This is the link in the chain that many people miss. They go after their goals, but secretly believe that they will not achieve them. They are lukewarm and passive instead of being on fire and aggressive. They lack confidence and continue to second-guess themselves due to fear and emotional baggage. You can manage your anger and you can accomplish your dreams if you decide to believe in yourself and God 100%.

Believability Scale

1_____ 2_____ 3_____ 4_____ 5_____ 6_____ 7_____ 8_____ 9_____ 10_____

On a scale of one to ten, one being the lowest and ten being the highest, circle the number that represents your belief that you can be successful in managing your anger. If you circle ten, that means you are very confident. If you circle one, that means that you are not confident.

1. Explain why you chose the number you circled.

_____

_____

_____

_____

_____

2. What can you do to increase your belief?

_____

_____

_____

_____

_____

ACCOUNTABILITY PARTNERS

Sometimes we need assistance in being accountable for our action or inaction. Accountability partners can help us stay on track with our goals by checking our progress. They tell us what we need to hear, not what we want to hear.

Accountability partners tell us the truth and are not enablers. They are invested in our long-term success. They can be friends, family members, co-workers, or members at church.

Write down the qualities of a great accountability partner.

_____

_____

_____

_____

_____

_____

_____

_____

_____

_____

_____

_____

_____

_____

Do you feel it is important for someone to hold you accountable?

Yes or No

Write down names of potential accountability partners who you trust to hold you accountable. Be careful in who you choose. Everyone is not meant to be an accountability partner. The person you choose may have great qualities, but may not be great in holding people accountable.

Potential Accountability Partners	What qualities do they have?

BE THANKFUL

We sometimes forget about our blessings and take them for granted. It is important to appreciate the things that we have. When you think about complaining always remember that things can be worse. Believe it or not, there are people in this world that wish they were in your position.

List the things that you are thankful for.

_____   _____

_____   _____

_____   _____

_____   _____

People take care of the things that they truly appreciate. For example, if someone appreciates their car, they keep their car clean and make sure that they keep up on the maintenance. Appreciation is more than saying words. It is consists of feeling thankful and doing things that show that you are appreciative. God blesses those that appreciate what they already have.

List the things that you can do to show your appreciation.

_____

_____

_____

_____

_____

_____

_____

_____

_____

_____

ANGER LOG

Week 1

Rank your anger on scale from one to ten. One being lowest and ten being highest.

1   2   3   4   5   6   7   8   9   10

Please explain your ranking for this week

_____

_____

_____

_____

_____

Week 2

Rank your anger on scale from one to ten. One being lowest and ten being highest.

1   2   3   4   5   6   7   8   9   10

Please explain your ranking for this week

_____

_____

_____

_____

_____

_____

_____

_____

Week 3

Rank your anger on scale from one to ten. One being lowest and ten being highest.

1   2   3   4   5   6   7   8   9   10

Please explain your ranking for this week

_____

_____

_____

_____

_____

Week 4

Rank your anger on scale from one to ten. One being lowest and ten being highest.

1   2   3   4   5   6   7   8   9   10

Please explain your ranking for this week

_____

_____

_____

_____

_____

Week 5

Rank your anger on scale from one to ten. One being lowest and ten being highest.

1   2   3   4   5   6   7   8   9   10

Please explain your ranking for this week

_____

_____

_____

_____

_____

Week 6

Rank your anger on scale from one to ten. One being lowest and ten being highest.

1   2   3   4   5   6   7   8   9   10

Please explain your ranking for this week

_____

_____

_____

_____

_____

Week 7

Rank your anger on scale from one to ten. One being lowest and ten being highest.

1   2   3   4   5   6   7   8   9   10

Please explain your ranking for this week

_____

_____

_____

_____

_____

Week 8

Rank your anger on scale from one to ten. One being lowest and ten being highest.

1   2   3   4   5   6   7   8   9   10

Please explain your ranking for this week

_____

_____

_____

_____

_____

Week 9

Rank your anger on scale from one to ten. One being lowest and ten being highest.

1   2   3   4   5   6   7   8   9   10

Please explain your ranking for this week

_____
_____
_____
_____
_____
_____

Week 10

Rank your anger on scale from one to ten. One being lowest and ten being highest.

1   2   3   4   5   6   7   8   9   10

Please explain your ranking for this week

_____
_____
_____
_____
_____
_____

Week 11

Rank your anger on scale from one to ten. One being lowest and ten being highest.

1   2   3   4   5   6   7   8   9   10

Please explain your ranking for this week

_____
_____
_____
_____
_____
_____

Week 12

Rank your anger on scale from one to ten. One being lowest and ten being highest.

1   2   3   4   5   6   7   8   9   10

Please explain your ranking for this week

_____

_____

_____

_____

_____

_____